A Soldier's Daughter

A Soldier's Daughter

Poems by Lois Brown Klein

Turning Point

Published by Turning Point
P.O. Box 541106
Cincinnati, OH 45254-1106

ISBN: 9781934999004
LCCN: 2008901431

Poetry Editor: Kevin Walzer
Business Editor: Lori Jareo

Visit us on the web at www.turningpointbooks.com

Cover Art Photograph: Marisa Allegra Williams
Cover Design: Jenny Mountjoy

Acknowledgments

"Naming Water" appeared in *The Lucid Stone*

"Braille" was first printed in *Crowd*, poetry magazine of the New School of NY, and subsequently in *The Santa Barbara Independent*

"Without" appeared in *The Star* (newsletter of the American World War II Orphans Network) and *Drumvoices Review* and is forthcoming in *Spillway*

"A Family Minus One" was recently published in *The Star*

"The Real Story" appeared in *Rivertalk*

"Mere Ink" and "Vanished" (under the title of "Night Vision") appeared in *The South Carolina Review*

"Into the Ark" appeared in *Confluence*

"Braids" is forthcoming in *Creative Writing in Four Genres* (edited by David Starkey; Bedford/St. Martins Press)

I am grateful to Larry Smith and Beth Berlese, who brought life to my words, and to Ellen Kelley and Barry Spacks who brought the music. My heartfelt thanks also to my friends, too many to mention here, for their enduring support and belief in me. And to my family for accompanying me on this road.

for my father

Major Ira Brown
1906-1942

U.S. Army Medical Corps

Table of Contents

"Art is a house that wants to be haunted."

Marianne Moore

Part One

The Real Story

To leave her something
worthier of blame
they told my mother
it was sabotage.

This is the real story.

Imagine it: the barracks at night
cots with khaki blankets
one man smokes a cigarette
his eyes slowly closing

a spark falls
orange snake of flame
digs at wool, sears the sheets
races up old wood walls
devours the air
illumines the pale hapless faces

and the smoke
presses down on everything
on men too sunk in sleep to rouse—
perhaps even then dreaming
of evenings by a campfire
as the heavy drift of smoke
sings in their lungs
sings them to sleep.

The child isn't told

her father is gone.
She had learned to walk
but returns to crawling.
She can no longer bear
the thought of falling.
A doctor is consulted,
finds nothing wrong.

Back Porch

The porch, gray slatted
in the brittle sun,
pocked with crusted snow
dreary with city soot—

a small corral for the little girl
set down for fresh air,
out from under mother's feet.
In snowsuit and mittens
she looks around,
then pounds her muffled fists
against the door and cries
to be let in—

only the rattle and clack
of the elevated train, the sharp
bark of a neighbor's dog,
the winter wind that bites
her nose and cheeks.
In a frozen voice
she sings her magic-song,
the one that's supposed
to make her mother come.

Transported

Through the tall windows
shafts of sunlight
pierce the dimness
of our living room.
I call them streamliners,
like those trains
other fathers take to work.
I like to watch
the dust motes float
and slowly rise
in the bright slanted paths.
I pretend each tiny wisp
is a body
on its way to heaven—
a way to keep believing
people do not
simply disappear.

On the Cover of Look Magazine

A few photographs remain,
most posed in his khaki uniform

except this one
on the cover of Look magazine—

March, 1940—a close-up of his head
in surgeon's mask and cap

bent over a newborn's waxy face.
His gloved hand squeezes

drops of silver nitrate
into the newly opened eye—

a first in medicine
that made him a legend,

this father who lived so briefly
in his own child's vision.

Braids

Mother gripped my hair to wind in braids
her blue-veined hands cool and deft
as if remembering a shadow time:
Her fault the man had left.

Her blue-veined hands cool and deft
against my forehead when I lay ill.
Her fault the man had left,
her old mistakes regretted still.

Against my forehead when I lay ill
striped sunlight through venetian blinds.
Her old mistakes regretted still,
no defense could ease the pain.

Striped sunlight through venetian blinds
like prison bars enclosed my world.
No defense could ease the pain.
Braided hair bound tight my curls.

Prison bars enclosed my world.
Mother's hands that twirled and gripped
my hair tight against my head.
No strand escaped or ever slipped.

Mother's hands that gripped and twirled,
hands that seemed both charmed and cruel.
My hair tight against my head
yet she would place a ribbon there.

Her hands that seemed both charmed and cruel
as if remembering a shadow time,
yet she would place a ribbon there
despite the way she gripped my hair.

We tried to think

we were lucky. No—
that's a lie. We never did
think that. The three of us
little girls with just a mother.

But we had an imaginary
family—Daddy and Evie Levy
and Gentian Violet—
pretend-people to care for
and make believe they cared for us.

One day our mother came in
sat on the toy chest.
Get off! Get off!
You're squishing Evie Levy!
Not a part of our game
she left the room
and the space closed behind her.

Lincoln Park Zoo, 1944

Polished white shoes
   laces washed and bleached
three small girls throw
   marshmallows to Mike the polar bear

wind their fingers through
   the cyclone fencing meant
to protect them from wild things
   beg their mother for cotton candy

while Mike curls his black tongue
   around another white puff
and Mother scans the crowd
   for would-be kidnappers

holds their hands so tightly
   they whine and pull away
Mike's tongue lolling, fur dulling
   with soot in the sullen afternoon.

Uncle Max

A woolen blanket, a hearing aid,
Uncle Max's thick fingers
and whispered voice, the window
framing darkened fields.

The memory whirls, unlocks words—
kneel, shoulder, buckle—none certain.
The old black porter readies
our upper berth, closes the heavy

canvas curtains with us inside.
The rhythm of the train,
the clack of wheel against rail,
a hum of aftershave.

Unpacking

I am seven, cross-legged
on the linoleum floor
surrounded by cardboard boxes
and crumpled newsprint.

Mother has moved us
to four sad rooms above a pool hall.
It is my job to arrange the kitchen.
I want to do it right.

I decide to put the tea-towels
and the aprons, all the soft things,
together. I wonder if the spoons
should go with the bowls.

Like words set down too carefully
on a page, I stack the plates
one on top another, facing the mute
blue flowers all the same direction.

Sorry

I imagine he scoops me up into his arms.
  I feel the smoothness of his palm,
    the wool of his uniform against my leg.

Maybe he is asking or telling me something
  when I see the dog across the room
    and wriggle to get down. He holds me tight.

Perhaps he's smoothing down my curls or
  breathing the clean scent of baby shampoo.
    Maybe he is saying good-by.

My white lace-up shoes rest against
  his hip, my dress flowers across his hand—
    when finally I twist away and down.

My skin still feels the pressure of his arm
  even as he frowns and walks away,
    followed by the dog.

A Family Minus One

Wrapped in cotton batting,
each of us drifted through
our four small rooms,
our separate dreams and sorrows.
Like pupae, frail and faltering,
eyes squeezed shut
to the world which had stolen
our husband-father-soldier
and never returned him.
Afraid to say the only things
we needed to say,
our pale bodies shared a space,
our hearts sealed in silence.

My Ninth Summer

What is long past
could have been yesterday:
a humid evening,
a game of kick the can.

Kids scatter to hiding places,
I to the hayloft with its silence
and musty smells, the dusty air
peeling from walls and bales.

I burrow against the hay,
gritty bits sticking to my face.
I am thinking of my father,
his death growing in me
until it is so huge I cannot move.

I am curled around a pain
there is no name for in my world,
pray that my stillness
will keep it from being seen.

Shouts and laughter below,
metal clank of can,
the ollie-ollie-oxen-free
that calls us in.

Mother

When I asked her
for a dog or even ice cream
she'd say *we'll see*
when all I wanted was a yes
would even settle for no
just to be sure of something
in my child's world

Later, when words themselves
meant less than her stance
hands on hips
I learned *we'll see* was immutable
a permanent condition
to avoid any decision
as she stood in the kitchen
treading water—unable
to go forward yet determined
not to go under

Homesick

In shorts
and halter tops
we spill
down
the wide stairs
to the cinnamon-toast
kitchen.
Holy, Holy, Holy,
Early in the morning
sung in little-girl
voices,
we rush to finish
breakfast
the sooner to wait
the hour
before splashing
into the clear
pebble-edged lake.

Clasping
my tattered
Secret Garden,
I head for
the porch that
wraps
like an apron
around the great house
to the swing

whose frayed blue
cushions
nestle me,
the wooden cradle of it
silver-smooth
against my bare legs,
it's gently creaking
ropes
the holiest
of music.

We have our
own secret,
the porch swing and I:
I whisper
to it my sadness
and it rocks me.

End of a Beach Day

The day is over and all that waits
is the dark interior of a house,
the what-shall-I-make-for-dinner,
the sand finding its inevitable way
into every clean corner, and the long
evening stretching out into shadow.

So call the children from the waves,
rinse pails and shovels, pack up scraps
of sandwiches, shake out the damp
blanket, fold it across and across again,
begin the weary journey home.

Uncle Sonny

Oh, he could laugh at things
and make us laugh—
once he led us
through the house, jumping
over chairs and couches,
shod in muddy boots
while his tidy wife hissed
You're a crazy man!

In an old photo, I am thirteen,
sedate in their living room
at some family gathering—
a bored, unhappy face
above my skirt and sweater,
neck scarf neatly tied

as though I were waiting
for something to be over
and something else to start.

Flirting

never did work out for me
I never had the flair
for sauciness and teasing

I watched other girls
smile their slow smiles,
drawl a clever line with ease

They had honed their style
with fathers at supper tables
all across our town

They had space to make mistakes,
knew you win a few
and lose a few, the game goes on

But for me, each word swallowed,
each smile suppressed,
felt a matter of life or death

Fathers' Hands

I notice other fathers' hands—
the strong tanned ones
that lift a child from the swing

the gentle ones that cradle
a baby's tender head
palm snug against the downy skull

the steadfast ones gripped
by a trusting toddler
taking her first uncertain steps.

I don't remember my father's hands.
I imagine them fair-skinned
and freckled, nails white like moons.

I know they wore surgeon's gloves
birthed babies when the phone calls came
gave me a bottle at 5 a.m.

They even learned to crochet
(just to prove he could my mother said)
and play an awkward game of tennis.

I have to believe my father's hands
traced the curve of my infant ear
brushed my wispy towhead hair

tied careful bows on my white shoelaces
swung me high in the autumn air.

The Expedition

Parka sugared with snow, schoolbooks
in hand, I see my mother on the old
nubby couch, her nylonned legs stretched
out, feet absently scritch-scritching
against each other. She is climbing
Mt. Everest with Sir Edmund Hillary.

The air in the room feels all used up,
as if at a great altitude. I see her face, pale
with winter, framed in faded auburn hair
thinned from a life of worry and doubt—yet
remarkably composed in the feeble
afternoon light scaling the square glass panes.

Her head is thrust forward as though
she were part of the expedition.
My arrival is not enough to bring her home.
She turns the pages with a hunger
that maddens me. Yet I know without them
she might leave us altogether.

Maidenhair

Row on row of fragile disc-shaped leaves
lined up like eager children at their desks,
long fronds that dip and sway with every breeze,
their soft green skirts bowing as I pass.

Something about them inspired and newborn,
each tiny leaf a round mouth surprised to find
all those others showing off this very form
like forest pearls strung along a graceful line.

Not meant to be indoors, confined in pots
they never fail one day to brown and curl,
each tender leaf dried to a dark green dot,
what was once alive now of the netherworld.

Like dominoes falling, they cannot be retrieved,
another living thing we learn to grieve.

Missing Him

Layers of rain blur
the long arms of oaks,
rattle the stiff leaves.
Evening gathers iron-gray.
A woman broods over
a photograph—out of focus
since the day it was taken.

The constant *plink*
of raindrops in the metal gutter
is making her crazy—
she struggles to focus on
a single ragged leaf
twisting round and round
on its thin stem—
waits for it to tear away, and fall.

My Mother's Birthstone

In the psych ward
                    she sat amid
a bewilderment of garnets—

rings, bracelets, pendants
crafted by
                    her roommate's son.
She had written a check for them all.

Now she was smiling.
Her doctor loved her,
                    she told me,
displaying a stone on her finger

the stone of blood and fire.

Discovery

Roadside blackberries—
a thousand thorny branches
wind their summer lives
together, five-petalled flowers
a feral bank of snow.

Stepping in to pick—
ankles bare and pricked
we are swallowed by blackberries
our purple mouths brushing
the darkness below the light.

Part Two

Naming Water

*"...to come out of the prison of silence,
where no tone of love, no song of bird,
no strain of music ever pierces the stillness...."*
                              Helen Keller

This scene always made me weep,
waiting as I was for my own miracle,
for someone who would release me
from a different sort of silence,
for someone to touch my face
and teach me—

a teacher unafraid of wildness,
otherworldly grunts,
unnerving cries, who every day
dipped my hand in water
and made the word for water
next to it on my skin, who held
unwilling fingers to her throat
to feel the word ripple
across vocal cords rising and falling.
And then one day, after the long
journey to trust, realizing
that touch was the word for water,
that water could be named
between two people, could be
asked for and received.

Someone

I have wanted to belong to someone,
my life secured to his, two ships
bound to find new land or tip
off the edge of the world, together.
It suited me to put my trust in another.

This needing to be someone's, it's old,
deep in the folds of my gray brain,
the skin on my neck where I dab perfume,
crouched in the soles of my feet
and woven round this thickening waist.

I tell my body, forget this vestigial longing—
but comes the sigh, the tears, and again
it swells, this thing that marks me.

Since Then

It is the shadow of what we were
so long ago that returns again
in the electric whisper
of a lover's mouth on my neck.
I lean into him and tumble backward
to a dream of being that small bundle
against my father's shoulder—
he bends to brush his whiskered face
against the unclothed space between
my ear and gown and I breathe in
the scent of lemon and springtime—
breathe it into every cell
where it has stayed almost dormant
since then—since the war and the fire
the letter from President Roosevelt
my mother's ocean of sadness.

Intruder

A pant leg disappearing
off the edge of my dream—cuffed khaki,
a plain dark shoe against black shadows.
I am shouting at my two small grandsons
vanishing in a pool of midnight water
You must not go in there alone!
shouting because I cannot see them.

And there it hangs. I wake shaking,
terrified of the blackcold deep.

When I was little, just barely walking,
I must have seen that same pant leg
a hundred times before it turned the corner
and was gone. *Died* was the word I later
heard linked with father. But I could not say it.
I learned to write *Deceased* on the necessary forms,
a word with distance built into it. Not like
died or dead. Not like a pant leg disappearing.

Without

Without a father,
without the way he kneels beside his toddler
to explain the petals on a flower

Or the way he says *let's go for a ride,
just us two* and opens the car door
like Atticus in *To Kill a Mockingbird*

Without the treasures he might bring:
ribbons for my hair, socks with frilly tops,
a Canadian quarter, a blue jay feather

Without his arm around my shoulder
as we unravel a math problem or I model
the dress I'm wearing to the prom

But mostly without the smile that fathers
save for their daughters,
the smile that teaches me to smile.

Letters Home, 1941

After many years I found (again)
Dad's letters to my mom, penned on
Camp Grant stationery—a generosity of paper.
They wrote nearly every day,
bits of news, advice, requests—
all stranded on the page, the sentences
stalwart but bare, like some unfurnished room.

Scarcely any news here
Everything is going along ok
Will bring some neosynephrin home with me
The camp is getting busy
I hope Na is feeling better now
Tell Minnie that any cathartic is no good for her
I hope you had fun at the party on Saturday
Find enclosed the lease, a letter from Putsy,
    and a card from NY for Na
Everything is going along smoothly
Gosh, if I had only known that you would call
I want you to pay particular attention to
    the following: send me Aunt Clara's address
The work is getting more difficult
Yesterday we admitted over 200 patients
Just keep the rubber stocking on all the time
Don't take any chances
Please forgive me about the scolding
Rumor has it we may leave camp a week early
Kiss the babies
I am very anxious to have you here
The weather is still plenty hot

Mail my film out right away
We are all packed and set to start on the convoy
Kiss the babies for me
Love to you and all the gang
x x x x x x x x x x x x

Only now I find it strange—
the white moth of tenderness barely flickering
among black-inked words.

Until today I've never said

I'm Lois, Ira Brown's daughter,
out loud or to myself, have
never claimed my dad that way.
Even the word Father
seems to stand alone
floating on some surreal sea
beckoning from a distant
lighthouse in a country
forever unknown to me, a land
that most belonged to Mother
who would not take me there,
her tears a tribute to their love
which she held close,
while I survived outside
whatever light he shed.

Sisters' Visit

The last time they were here
together, my two sisters,
was never.

Since the early years
when we whispered mysteries
and made up an imaginary
family to help us forget our own,
we have struggled to be close,
to somehow reach each other.

The river of our loss
had stranded us, each in our own
silence, unable to cross.

In our 50's now, I wonder
what we'll talk about.
Our children and grandchildren,
jobs and health, no doubt.
And then?

There is so much to say,
a torrent of unvoiced words,
if only we can get beyond
our fear of drowning.

Flight

The plane lifts from the tarmac
nimbly as a child's balloon,
its scrap of shadow floating
over the quilted ocean.
Our flight attendant's voice lingers
Your nearest exit may be behind you
but that must be merely a formality
on this day when the baby
in the next row is already asleep
and the air is calm as church
and the smiling man beside me
doesn't talk too much or too little.
His sweatered elbow is easy
on the armrest, his long legs settled
into abbreviated space.
Breathing in the crisp of his cologne
I wish this were the home
I was headed to.

Simple Things

Today, the simplest things bring me to tears—
a white blouse fluttering from the clothesline

the way my cat's fur warms and calms my hand
the cry of a hawk, jagged, compelling

my own reflection in the bathroom mirror
dappled patch of sunlight on the kitchen table

the way the yellow couch cushions lean
unworried into one another.

Still Life

Heavy and still as the air
I sleep stretched out
on a damp sheet
through the hot afternoon
silent except for
the whispers of birds
among leaves never stirring.
The heat wraps around me
slows me
until each frame of my life
stands alone
and the no one next to me
comes into focus
a blank gray space
just me there wondering
how life has emptied out
to nothing
but the wish to sleep.

Into the Ark

*"An endless rain is just beginning.
Into the ark, for where else can you go…"*
            Wislawa Szymborska

Would they even let me in
without an other?
Is my one self enough to save?

Images of two-by-two's loom—
the elephants, shoulder to massive shoulder,
the tigers' matching stripes, kangaroos
hopping and tortoises plodding up the plank.

Even the twin crocodiles and scorpions,
mosquitoes, wasps and rattlesnakes
creep with all their cousins
toward the shelter of the ark.

And Noah himself, standing large
and urgent on the deck, has a wife below
apron'd and babushka'd
organizing food and beds for all.

I feel the rain begin.
My feet slip on the belly of the earth.
Two black ants dance in
just as Noah pulls up the ramp.

The Cat Who Refused
to Tie Her Shoes

Inca has a cat door she has learned to use
when I am not around. But let her get
a whiff of me and she meows loudly
to be let out. *Use the cat door* I insist
from behind my newspaper or
over my coffee cup. Still she sits, forlorn.

When I was little, I struggled to tie
my shoes. Mother showed me how
over and over until my stumbling fingers
could make the laces resemble a bow.
Later, when she was busy folding laundry
or washing dishes, I ached

for her soft face down close to mine,
her soothing scent, her smooth hands.
But she waved me off
with the same voice so familiar to my cat
Come now, you can do that.

Rorschach

In my inkblot midnight
the embittered woman
looms above her child

rules imposed
rules broken
the strong arm
the wooden spoon
endless Sundays
muted sky

something finished
never finished
comes to me with
its hundred dark mouths.

Weeds

Mother, today
weeding the flower bed
I thought of how
I've carried you, like

the endless weight
of weeds, their insistent green
bursting through the soil
after every rain

crowding
the fragile narcissus,
spreading their eager seeds,
overrunning beauty.

The Sometime Landscape

In the mornings when the fog-dimmed
trees shimmer into clarity
and the sun charms the gingko leaves,
the fragile song of sparrows
weaves a net of possibility I wear
like a shawl against the cool aloneness

of afternoon. Sun behind trees,
giant shadows reach across the lawn
like the family of my childhood.
Then dusk fades it all to black and white,
like a photograph from long ago
that will not come back to life.

My Father's Ghost

My father's ghost is everywhere.

He is the bullet I dodge,
the land mine I tiptoe around.

All the men on earth
come trooping along with him

in their uniforms of distress
with their smiles and bayonets.

They could invade at any hour.
I'm readying my armor.

Ruby Slippers

If I could gather all the stories
I've read into one vast room
and walk from each to each,
diving into the Charles
with Mr. and Mrs. Mallard, telling
the Pokey Little Puppy that he,
of all the puppies, had it right,
sitting on Winnie the Pooh's
lap as he sat for years on mine,
spooning honey with our paws,
marching down Mulberry Street
with its glorious imagined
parade, asking Curious George
if he ever missed the jungle—
then on to bigger books,
gossiping with Meg and the other
little women, spending two years
before the mast, happily whitewashing
Tom Sawyer's fence, and of course
wandering down the yellow brick road
with the tin man, that fellow who
didn't think he had a heart,
like me doubtful of his insides,
needing someone else to show him
and then still needing to believe it.

Undone

Sometimes
I feel like my body
hasn't followed
the recipe
Something never
came to a full boil
Certain spices
were forgotten
The pan
was the wrong size
So I turned out warm
on the outside
but still a little cool
in the middle.

Transference

He will always be
that one moment of entering his office,
the past week waiting in my throat,
the words lodged there
as I stared at the Oriental carpet
with its parade of silly maroon roosters—
what I came in to out of the cold.

He will always be that one moment
when the hour was up
and we both knew it without looking
and I hesitated by his chair,
wanting to touch his sleeve, take
the feel of his wool jacket home with me,
take something solid of him
home with me.

Indestructible Seed

Place one between your teeth
pluck off the stem
suck the purple globe

into the cavern
of your remembering—
open the fruit slowly

allow the thick juice
the crisp yielding of flesh
summer sweet

until just the pit is left—
that indestructible seed
to mull smooth within your cheek.

Cows on Hot Springs Road

I have come to breathe the heady earth of pasture,
the trampled mud between patches of green,
the grassy hillside rolling down
to a road hidden by hedgerow and eucalyptus.
I have come to stare at the plain faces of cows.

The two stand passive, brown and white coats
wrapped snugly over the hulk of shoulders
and rumps, over the patient knees.
Their tails hang still and damp from rain.
Both turn bulky heads toward me
as if viewing an undistinguished painting.

I have come to rest in the presence of cows,
whose very dumbness comforts me.
I hang on the wide slats of fence
and stare at the blank bovine faces,
the ache of me melting in the brown of their eyes.

Unsaid Things

Father, today on the trail
I hear you
in the slide and chuckle
of creek water
over stout mossy boulders.

You hover like the hum
of insects on this day
full of autumn,
your voice murmuring
you didn't want to go.

I listen for other unsaid
things, imagine they glide down
from the wide sky like
rusted sycamore leaves
sighing their way to the ground.

Symmetry

I like landscapes that happen
by accident—no thoughtful architect
with T-square and straight edge
bent on symmetry.

Give me trees with branches
helter-skelter, warped woodland paths
conceived by deer and hound,
rocks tossed willy-nilly in creek beds.

Yet my mind veers toward
the straight-forward,
pursues the shortest route,
loves knowing where I'll land,

holds to strict design,
'though no one's left to scold me
for tearing up the plan.

Breaking the Code

Hawks are writing
messages in the sky
(what we always thought
were lazy circles are not)

Look closely, you'll see
the arc of *e*, swoop of *y*,
double loop of *m*
across the page of blue

Is it our names
their bodies inscribe?
Some ancient tale? Or how
to speak when words fail?

Vanished

Over the quiet lane, black-limbed trees
arch like prayers in the dim moonlight.

From the dark shell of my car, something
live and luminous in a roadside puddle:

a barn owl, his round eyes wide,
as though mirroring my surprise.

A long moment hangs between us—
then his great wings unfurl and

lift in one smooth slow motion,
slip without sound into darkness

a flair of cream and amber feathers,
a rain puddle vacant and shining as an eye.

Braille

My small grandson
sleeps curved against me, his face
placid as the moon. With my hands,
I seek to memorize his perfect body—
feathery hair, boy-muscle of calf
and bicep, the track of his vertebrae—
so that years later I can summon up
every detail in my fingertips.

This started long ago,
this learning by heart the bodies of all
the men I slept beside. Not so much to recall
the particulars of them after their leaving,
but as a ritual in Braille, another way
of knowing them if ever they came back,
if ever I had to be sure of them in the dark.

The Time of Half-Awake

I used to like being half-awake
curled under woolen covers
when I would imagine my world
like a play—give myself a father,
an easy-going brother or two,
my own bedroom with a closet
full of cashmere sweaters
and real leather penny loafers,
a mother who baked bread
and listened to Sinatra.
Then I'd hear the bathroom faucet,
my mother's crooked cough
with the day's first cigarette.

Today I rise early,
leave the warm burrow of my bed
and the arms of my dreams.
Spooning coffee into the pot,
I find myself humming
Out of the tree of life
I picked me a plum,
mm-mm, mm, mm-mm, the best
is yet to come.

Faith

Damp sand unfolds

to ocean's lip.

Above, five pelicans

emerge from mist

almost

like a magic trick.

Single file they glide

soundless

at the edge of light

then slip back

into fog—

subtract themselves

from sight.

A Gentle Season

There is an ease of mind now
like being alone on a boat at sea,
a drifting quality of no-care,
a shrugging off of humdrum duties.

I am snug in my redwood house
on its small ocean of land.
A few remaining dried leaves
pin the solemn sky in place.
There is a gentleness to my season
that does not require or demand.

Others stand on the far shore,
their shapes so distant I cannot tell
if they are facing toward me or away.

What Pleases Us

We have to learn what pleases us,
let the sun glint on desires
hidden behind doors shut early
and loud by people we trusted.
When I was small, on meadowlark
days, the field behind my house
waved golden grasses against my legs.
Sometimes I lay down flat
and shouted to the sky
my name, my name, *my name*.

So She's Got to Have…

"So she's got to have happiness,
she's got to have truth, too,
she's got to have eternity—
did you ever!" Wislawa Szymborska

The dead come back to life,
walk about the old familiar
streets, smile, buy a coffee,
drink the scent of eucalyptus.

I watch the father who
made me a place in this world.
Even in the dream
I dread awakening.

But, of course, I wake,
move heavy legs from under
heavy quilt, do the things
we do each morning—

warm water splashed on face
comb drawn through hair.
Changing before the mirror
I glimpse my naked bicep,

flex, then laugh out loud.
Not since I was eight and scolded
for being proud have I
made a full-on strong man pose.

Here on Earth

When it's no good
here on earth
I look up at the sky—
the weight of indigo
with its scattering
of stars like the square
of a childhood quilt
grown to cover us all.

Mere Ink

The mere ink of words
heals, spills across
the page like children's
laughter—ink ringing
like the last bell
on the last day of school,
skipping like stones
across water—ink pulling
words out of the deep
like gleaming fish
whose silvery scales
reflect the whole of it.

Biography

Lois Klein holds a BA in English Literature fromTufts University and an MA in Psychology from Antioch University. Her chapbook *Naming Water* was published in 1998. Her poetry has been printed or is forthcoming in numerous regional and national journals. She has given readings throughout California and has been a featured presenter at the San Luis Obispo and Santa Barbara Poetry Festivals.

Ms. Klein is co-organizer of the Santa Barbara Poetry Series and coordinates the monthly Santa Barbara Favorite Poems Project readings. She is a Fellow of the South Coast Writers Project and teaches through the California Poets in the Schools program.